the गॉद

jnaneshwarar

ISBN 979-8-88815-631-5

Introduction

At the outset, I want to make it clear that **there is only one thing that exists** and that has evolved into this vast, complicated, and diversified universe or universes. Scientists are progressively moving towards this thing that they call it as ultimate particle. Even some scientists call it as God particle. In fact, they are searching for the ultimate particle that is **insentient**. They can move up to this level only and not to the level of **it's make up with sentient thing** involving some intermediate, unknown, and inexplicable steps. We must first understand that the **basic concept of creation is by combination or aggregation with or without physical or chemical or both the interactions of invisible smaller particles to form bigger visible particles** that we see around us in the universe. This concept ensures the dismantling of everything in the universe into its constituent ever existing invisible ultimate unit particle.

Such formations by combinations usually occur with changes in properties. Thus, the universe was created successively by combination. Any simultaneous process or processes might have also occurred with successive steps. However, the speed of creation would have been unimaginably faster.

What is that **sentient or conscious thing** that makes up the **insentient unit particle?** That ultimate sentient unit particle is none but **Life (in the form of Atman).** It is the **Being.** For understanding purpose, we can call it as **Life** 'particle'. Life is consciousness. To be exact, Life is knowledge. I think you cannot point out anything, in this universe, other than Life as conscious one. **If anything is said to be conscious in the universe, then, it must be due to Life or that associated with Life.**

If the universe, as strongly believed by scientists, is considered to have evolved only from **an ultimate unit particle,** it must be the Life 'particle' because this is the only particle that **truly exists** and hence, the existence of insentient ultimate particle is ruled out automatically. As it is believed that this universe has evolved from an ultimate unit particle, there is no question of two particles (separate sentient and insentient particles) evolving into this universe. Hence, the insentient things should have been formed or blossomed (indirectly as the nail, hair, and horns in living beings) from the sentient 'Life' particles. I want to say that this may be one of the ways by which insentient things are formed (only for the understanding purpose, it is given as analogy) and, who knows, it may involve some other mechanism that may remain unknown forever.

This infinitely small invisible singularity (Life particle) at the time of creation of the universe, became Atman (a light or fire form) first and then grew by combination, within no time, into an infinitely dense and hot huge pillar with reasonable as well as determined thickness extending on both extremities to an infinite length within the Space. This is termed by the great siddhar Kagapusundar as endless **fire pillar** and he says it as Linga form. This formation of fire pillar was followed by revolution (spinning) and detachment with explosion into pieces of varying sizes of different composition (with respect to five gross elements namely ether, air, fire, water, and earth) with positioning and further continuous inherent activities forming the cosmos which comprises the entire insentient beings or things. This seems to reflect the **Big Bang theory** put forward. But who knows the exact ways of creation of the universe?

We must also understand that **a lone sentient being (i.e., a Life particle in the form of Atman) unites with the so-called insentient beings or things in the form of food and grows into a bodied living being.** Thus, this world is made **lively with moving (living) beings** and **lovely with non-moving (living) beings.** Whatever we call as **it, he, and she** are none but the forms of Life (which are subsequently named differently by different languages) in this universe.

Life is versatile in all respects and even in the respect that we think to be never possible. That is, there is nothing impossible for it. It is eternal. What departs a living body leaving it dead is Life or Atman and that everybody knows. This departure of Life itself is a proof for its eternity. This eternity also proves 'rebirth'. There are so many living beings in this universe and it proves the existence of Life 'particles' in plural i.e., the existence of innumerable Life particles. Further, it fills the Space and forms the insentient things. How can we know the number of Life particles?

Is it possible to know the number by any means? Alas! Moreover, it is self-creating or expanding.

I am sure that I am not blathering or blabbering. I may seem to be a bit of philosopher in this book. This you can understand, if you fully read this book. To be frank, I, **with the grace and direction of 'God'** in me, am just a complier of facts picked from various sources mostly from Vedas and the songs of **accomplished devotees** presenting in a simple and unambiguous language to dig out the truth. I have read the **Upanishads, Bible, and Quran** with deep thinking and, in them, I don't find any difference in the concept or definitions of God but in the rules and regulations framed and then, thrust for personal reasons (such as dominance) and gains and also for identity. If I get into details, you will just retire to a stream of questions in your mind. This presentation itself which you are going to find to be very brief, may also raise a lot of questions. However, I humbly say that it may reduce the number of questions to a greater extent and at the same time, make you to understand what the great thinkers have expressed in Vedas, messengers (such as Jesus Christ, Mohammed and others) in their revelations, and the devotees in their songs. Knowingly or unknowingly, **what has been given the name 'God' is none but Life** since Life, being conscious, is omnipresent, omnipotent, and omniscient.

Vedas, no doubt, is a treasure of knowledge but given, somewhat, in ambiguous words (with many different meanings). My humble opinion is that Vedas are not fully understood. Even the revelations of messengers are not correctly understood. Moreover, some explanations given by experts are contradictory and misleading. The real hidden meaning of Vedas or revelations is not correctly and fully explored. However, the hidden meaning, *especially of Vedas*, can be realized to some greater extent by going through the sayings of great saints such as Dattareya (a naked sage said to be an incarnation of three gods or simply Lord Vishnu) in his Avadootha gita, Vashista (who was the teacher of Rama in the epic, Ramayana) in his Yoga Vashista or Uttra Ramayana, and in the songs of true devotees. Though the Vedas have explicitly expressed about Brahman as Prana (i.e., Life), we have miserably missed to catch the meaning. As a result, Vedas and in particular, the appalling misunderstanding of pantheism of monism in Hinduism has become a platform for derisive criticisms.

Prana refers to living. Living is that which incarnates birth, (Direct incarnation involves only the appearance and disappearance or sometimes with growth for certain time period and disappearing) grows, and eventually passes or it is 'Being' or 'Existence'. Prana must principally and literally be taken as 'Life' or as a vital breath or principle that connects the living physical body (the individual) to the external world according to the context mentioned. When we sever this external connection by practice (not by death), the "Life" in the body will not depart. Once it is achieved, the individual who is now a realized Atman, may voluntarily discard the physical body. This can also be achieved by making the mind dormant (i.e., by not thinking and entering into acts). Being in this realized Atman stage, the individual is free to take any physical body and discard it at will (i.e., as he wishes) and can also have more than one physical body at the same time.

I want to stress that the intellectual philosophers on Upanishads of Vedas may point out that unless the three states of waking, dream, and deep sleep are considered with their significances, one cannot be adequately equipped for the enquiry into the ultimate truth (Life). This is the **matter still unknown** to or unexploited by the rest of the world. **The relation of mind to Life is another point** that has not as yet been even dreamt of by them. That is why the **Mandukya Upanishad**, which discusses the three states or expressions of human body, is considered to be the **epitome** of all Upanishads.

As regards the truth, everyone, even a fool, thinks that what he knows is the truth. It may be so in all other aspects such as religion, theology, mysticism, etc. But the philosophy of Vedanta (the ultimate truth or conclusion of Vedas) is something different. It starts and ends with the very fundamental thing Sat or Brahman (i.e., Life or Life in Atman state). Vedas often indicate Sat (or Being or Om) as 'Tat' ('Tat' means "that" without giving a name. hence, the Being is nameless.

All the Upanishads of Vedas just *stress to know your Atman or soul by meditating* on it. Meditating is to know the invisible Atman in you by materializing it. Materialization can be accomplished by the union of mind with Life or by the mercy of God. By this way, you sever the contact of your mind with the outside world and identify yourself with **the Atman magnified**

by its effulgence. By identifying and seeing (in fact realizing) your Atman, you come to know all other Atmans of individuals as well as the Atmans associated in insentient things creating the universe or you simply become cognizant of everything. In my opinion, *Vedas just reveal the truth. Hinduism, with its various beliefs, has unanimously adopted the Vedas.* Its truth is independent of sect, creed, color, race, sex, and various beliefs or religions.

God is not at all an illusion because Life is not an illusion or phantom. There is also a strong negation to the existence of God. How can we negate the existence of Life? Is not Life an incontrovertible proof? Whatever it is, whether anything will occur by chance or accident? Definitely, there is no chance. I think chance (or accident or even spontaneity) cannot be a cause for the creation of the universe because it may, invariably, lead to uncertainties and non-coherence as it is not conscious. Moreover, when chance is the cause or when the chance seems to be the cause, we need not stick to ethics, rules and regulations. This, in turn, may lead to chaos, pandemonium, and vandalism. Chance can be ruled out totally as there is some inherent harmony existing in the Nature itself and among the living beings.

*In my opinion, the greatest foolishness among human beings is to believe in different Gods, although they (pantheism) are all same (monism) with respect to Atman or soul (to be frank we believe in different names) and enter into wasteful arguments. Certainly, the belief in different Gods, without understanding the **oneness** among them, has brought in the present hatred infused environment or situation existing in this wonderfully created beautiful and harmonious world. This has also made the humans to **drift away from oneness**. I think, if we have entirely different Gods, I couldn't have a physical make-up with the same features as that of a Christian or of a Muslim or whether a Christian or a Muslim could have the same physical make-up as that of a Hindu? Invariably, selfishness and ego rule the roost.*

The God

Before the creation of this universe, we live in, Life called as **'Sat'** (Being) in Vedas, an absolute form of knowledge with full of bliss, occupying the Space, with no boundary, has existed into indefinite past. The universe was in a non-materialized state or the Life didn't appear in various forms we see now. Or, simply the universe was not created. Hence, Life is Space and Space is Life. In other words, Life in numerous discrete invisible, identical, and individual (or infinitesimal fractions of space) forms fills the Space presenting emptiness. It is the minute of the minutest with nothing smaller than this. Hence, there can be nothing to create it but it creates itself **and expands.** It can create everything by combination or by interaction or by both. It is the source for each and everything. It is the only thing existing in a blissful state. Initially the Space was absolute dark with no kind of motion. Therefore, Space is also termed as dark. **It was utmost calm and dark – an absolute peaceful state that cannot be described.** There were/are nothing but Life particles filling as dark Space presenting virtually a vacuum. In fact, there **exists no vacuum but a vacuum-like state.** Whenever the endless Space or space of the universe is mentioned, we must think as that filled with invisible Life 'particles' presenting the so-called vacuum. The same state will prevail when the universe (or universes) is dissolved.

In the beginning of indefinite past, as already mentioned, there was nothing in visible state but in invisible subtle state with no difference. At that state, what could have been the temperature? No one can say or even imagine. It can exist in that extreme cold temperature (*I doubt, whether the word 'temperature' is applicable to that state*) as well as in unimaginably extreme states on the opposite state i.e., at extremely highest temperature or it itself can take the form of fire. Simply, it can exist at any temperature. What is that existing in subtle state, as already said, is Life.

Before the creation of this universe, *there was nothing but the long lightless darkness and nothing visible existed.* There was no ether, no air, no fire, no water, and no earth. That means there were no elements such as hydrogen, oxygen, carbon etc. There was nothing like sound, touch, sight, taste, and smell. It was only **existence with no duality**.

Life (particle) is minute of the minutest and subtle of the subtler. It is unbelievably non-existing-like. Being invisible and subtle, it is indivisible. It is part-less whole. It is knowledge. It is unchanging. It is stainless and cannot be contaminated. It cannot be dried, wetted, or burnt out. It is absolute peace. It is spotless pure. It has no life but it is the Life for all living beings. It is bliss. It has no source by virtue of its size or its abstractness. It has no color, no ear, no eyes, no mouth, no nose, no hands or legs. Its form cannot be mentioned as this and that. It can never be seen and there is no base for it because it is the base for all. It is fearless. It is speechless. There is nothing like internal or external. It surpasses senses. It is not to be pointed out as this or that. It is ever existing one. At the same time, it is everything and there is nothing apart from it. There is nothing impossible for it. In simple words, it defies description, demarcation and its capabilities have no limit.

From the descriptions given above for Brahman (Sat or Life) by Vedas, one may brush it aside as rubbish or even laugh it off. But it is true. No one can deny with any reason because it is the only one that is wholesome in knowledge. It is **the only thing that remains uncontaminated** making the universe fantastically lively.

We all believe 'Life' exists. Then, we must accept the existence of 'God' because 'God' himself is Life. Life is none other than 'God'. 'God' is none other than Life. We know that when a living person dies, we say his Life (to be exact Life in Atman or soul state) is gone from his body and what is left behind is his dead body. When something goes out of the living body, the body is described as dead. Then, what is that something going out? That something which goes out is Life. Nobody has seen the Life going out. Yet, we know there is Life i.e., we accept the existence of Life. Here, we come to know about the unknown (i.e., Life) by knowing about the known (i.e., dead body). By this simple logical reasoning, the existence of Life can be proved beyond doubt. *It is the only method by which the existence of Life can be proved.* It remains and will **remain unknown for ever.** Hence, it becomes an undeniable fact that 'Life' exists, and hence, 'God' exists. Life is rightly called as Brahman (meaning vast and unlimited) by Vedas. **Life, knowledge, 'God', and Brahman point to the Being/Sat only**. Brahman is bliss. Life, Knowledge and Bliss are described in Vedas as Sat, Cit, and Ananda respectively. Sat means being/existence or Life. Cit means knowledge. Ananda means bliss. In other words, what exists is nothing but Knowledge. Knowledge itself is Being. Being (i.e., Life) is known along with or as knowledge. That is why its nature is bliss.

Upanishad also says that Atman is Truth. And the Truth of Truth is Life/knowledge with no proper name but only a name that describes it.

Yajnavalkya, a great sage of Vedic period was asked, *"Which is the one God"*. He replied, *"The Prana (Life); that is Brahman"* which is called as 'he 'and 'that' (that is why we refer Brahman as he or that) – (Brahadaranyaka Upanishad 3:9:9)

The great sage or siddhar by name Thirumoolar says, *"You find that there is one God for the world and that one, for the world, is Life"* - (Song 2962) And in another song, he says, *"God Shiva is Life"* - (Song 2822)

Brahman prepares itself for creation

When Brahman wanted to create the universe, it thought. Thinking is an inherent nature of knowledge. Though it is inherent, knowledge can remain without thinking. Thinking can be considered as the active part of knowledge. If knowledge/life does not think, nothing will come up or materialize. Nothing will come into existence visibly or invisibly. No action is possible. One may say, "I think". That means mind is born or comes into existence or we have given the name mind, for the act of thinking. But mind is subtle and at the same time *Maya*. (The other name for *Maya* is Sakthi or energy) which is depicted as **female** and the knowledge/Life 'particle' as **male**). What is *Maya*? *Maya* is, it exists or exists not. Mind is born when knowledge thinks. Mind does not exist (or is dormant) when knowledge does not do the act of thinking. Creation starts with the creation of mind. Then, the mind takes up the job of creation. That is, Brahman creates the universe through mind or Shakti. So, creation is solely a product of mind. By thinking, movement is caused followed by sound and light.

Creation cannot be lively without ups and downs. There must also be opposites for each and everything, may be in color, taste, smell, texture, size, shape, sound, light, character, behavior, etc. And for this, three gunas (or qualities) are imparted by knowledge/Life to mind. Knowledge/Life is independent but the mind is dependent. It depends on knowledge for its acts. The three gunas are **Sattva(m), Rajas, and Tamas**. These gunas are the primal constituents of Prakriti (mind), primordial nature, *natura naturans* from which the whole universe, physical and psychical (mental), has evolved.

"There is not an entity (individual) either on earth or in heaven (i.e., among Devas), that is liberated from these three gunas (qualities) born of mind (i.e., Prakriti)" – Bhagavad Gita: 18:40

Life, the only immutable and intelligent entity, is ever distinct from Prakriti and its evolutes – mind, organs, body, and external objects. All changes and all movements are in the realm of Prakriti and it is the very presence of Life that enables Prakriti to function and transform. The combination of Life and the mind impregnated with the gunas get the name Atman or Soul. *(These gunas themselves are **contradictory and complementary** with each other and at the same time working in unison. They mix in different* *proportions and grades to exhibit innumerable differences. These three gunas and their blends and the preponderance of anyone of these three gunas in varying degrees are the sole reasons for all types of differences in sentient beings as well as in insentient beings or things (in general, differences in all types of nouns).* Refer also the Chinese philosophical concept - **yin yang**)

Life is Brahman. Before creation or it becomes creations, it is termed as **pure Brahman**. Before Brahman enters into the act of thinking, the mind (a form of energy) is without liveliness or in a subdued state within pure Brahman. When it becomes lively because of thinking, it pervades Brahman (knowledge or Life) i.e., Brahman gets itself pervaded by mind or Shakti and the Brahman is termed as **para-Brahman**.

This mind, with no inherent nature, gets in the presence of Brahman, the unmodified three gunas namely Sattva, Rajas, and Tamas. The mind with pure Sattva guna is said to be in blissful state or form. The mind with pure Rajas guna is said to be in knowledge state. The mind with Tamas guna is said to be in existence state. When para-Brahman associates with blissful state of mind, it is said to suffer the deep sleep state. In this state, para-Brahman is termed as **Paramanandar** (in full bliss state). When Paramanandar associates with the knowledge form of mind, it is said to suffer the dream state and Paramanandar gets the name **Desomayar** (all effulgent). When Desomayar associates with existence form of mind, it is said to suffer the all-pervading waking state and is now termed as **Paripoornar** or simply **Poornar** (or **Poornam**).

Simply, Atman with these three states is termed as Poornam (or Poornar), *a perfect wholesome state of Life/Brahman for the purpose of creation.* Poornar is also called as **Satchithanandar** (*sat* means Existence/Life, *cit* means Knowledge, and *ananda* means Bliss). The mind then gets into modified state. The mind exclusively with Sattva guna, though in association with the other two gunas, is termed as *Maya*.

The size of Atman is same as that of Life. Vedas say Atman is subtler than subtle. This illumined Atman, though an ordinary human being cannot see, can be seen by great sages, saints or yogis. **Life can never be seen but the effulgence of Life in Atman state can be seen** (in fact realized) because the light that Atman emits makes it so many million times bigger than itself. That is why Atman is described variously to be the size of a grain of paddy, barley, mustard, or millet or even of thumb size (which are all can be seen by naked eye) in Upanishads. It is made to be of that size so as to be seeable by the great men of knowledge and that too with the power acquired to see **the effulgent Atman** by the grace of God.

(Note: Guna comprises a mixture of nature, character, behavior, quality, and their attributes put together. For more details, Bhagavad Gita may be referred. The attributes (including organoleptic properties such as color, taste, smell, and touch) of these gunas are

1. **Sattva**: Goodness, purity, constructive, harmonious, tendency of forgiving, forbearance and related qualities. It is the principle of poise conducive to purity, knowledge, and bliss.

2. **Rajas**: Passion, activity, heroism, tolerance, attachment, tendency of punishing and related qualities. It is the principle of motivity leading to activity, desire, restlessness, and disquietude.

3. **Tamas**: Ignorance, impurity, darkness, inertia, laziness, insentient nature, confusion, tendency to kill, and related qualities. It is the principle of inertia resulting in inaction, dullness, and delusion.)

The words Life (representing **neutral Brahman**) and Atman (representing **polarized Brahman**) are often times used interchangeably. However, the word Atman (Atman is called as **soul** or even as **spirit** in English) is widely used in Vedas because it is the (active or perfect) form for creation - be it sentient or insentient. **Life is subtle and unmanifest**. Atman is also subtle but manifest by its effulgence and becomes the fundamental whole or the building unit for the creation of the universe and whatever formed by combination of Atman is manifest. Thus, the subtle Atman becomes manifest visibly by combination. What is manifest in the interim state (i.e., when it exists as universe in visible and invisible forms) will again become unmanifest Life as Space in the end.

The Life with inert mind and without three gunas (or three mala(m)s i.e., taints) or the Life with dormant mind is termed as pure Atman. That is, An Atman without the influence of mind is a pure Atman. Atman with the mind of pure Sattva guna is also termed as pure Atman. (**Atman** is also termed as **Pranavam** or **Om** (or AUM) in Vedas - Refer Mandukya Upanishad).

When the mixture of three gunas becomes the attributes of mind, the Atman is said to be impure. In other words, the Atman with active mind impregnated with the blends of gunas is termed as impure Atman.

Vedas of India have given the name **Brahman** for Sat or Life as already said and the Vedas define Brahman as **Existence, Knowledge, and Bliss.** What a beautiful, wonderful, and simple consummate definition! **Knowledge must be always in a state of Bliss since bliss is its nature.** It always remains to be an observer or witness in everything.

Prana (Life) *is Brahman, Ka* (joy or bliss) *is Brahman, Kha* (ether) *is Brahman.* – (Chandogya Upanishad *4:10:4).* [It is said, in Chandogya Upanishad, that Life = Brahman = joy or bliss = ether (Space or space). Ether is Brahman because Life particles fill the Space and so becomes the space (ether), a part of Space]. Thus, there is no happiness or joy in anything finite. Only the infinite is happiness.

Atman

Know that, even so being left by the living-self, this body surely dies but the living-self does not die. That (living-self) is Atman. – Upanishad.

You know, the dead body loses all its consciousness because of the departure of Atman in it and hence, we can say, now, Atman is a conscious thing. In this universe, the only conscious thing is nothing but Atman. **Can you think of anything else which is self-conscious other than Atman (or Life)? But, alas, it can also become insentient being with the consciousness curtailed or cut off. And that means sentient things can become insentient things and *vice versa*.** A living person has *some* knowledge and how does he get it? It is only from his Atman. We can say ***knowledge is expressed as consciousness inherent with perception***. When we consider Atman, it is better to describe it as a form of consciousness. Life is knowledge and Atman is consciousness. Simply, Atman is knowledge or consciousness as they can be used interchangeably.

You may have come to know a person who had been declared dead by doctors reverted to life and got up. What do you understand by this?

The Atman that had departed its body should again have entered the dead body to make it live. You would have read also about the experiences of those who were almost dead and came back to life. Such stories are prevalent in all parts of the world. You would have also heard about those who remembered their previous births. What does it mean? It means that the body has an end but not the Atman confirming that Life has no end and it exists for ever. Atman may enter into some other body when it is made to take rebirth.

We, now, know that Atman exists. It is simple logic that Atman **moves not** when it is residing in a living body and **it moves** when it leaves a living body. But, has anybody seen it? Has anybody, in so many millions of years, reported to have seen Atman moving out of the body? The answer will be an emphatic '**NO**'. Why nobody has seen it? That is because of its size. But to our astonishment, a great siddhar (a person who had realized himself), by name Thirumoolar, has given the size of Atman, which is almost subtle, in his Thirumandirum containing four lined songs (song number 2011) *approximately since he himself must have known that it is not possible to be exact.* How can anyone know such a small size? It may be through the grace of "God". As far as I know, nobody, in this world, has given the size as Thirumoolar in his Thirumandirum. Thirumoolar has given the size using the cow's hair on its back. Even in 19th century a great sage by name Ramalinga Adigal has given the size using the photon of light as $1/10000000$th size of a photon particle. Vedas of India has also given the size indirectly as subtle of the subtler. Let us not dwell on other's statement but just concentrate on Thirumoolar's statement of Atman (indirectly Life) size because he has (although approximately) specifically mentioned.

Before we know the size as given by Thirumoolar, it is better to know scientifically the nature of a very minute particle. It is quite interesting to know what is said about *Planck's length. Planck's length is said to be roughly about 1.6×10^{-35} meter at which the classical ideas about gravity and space-time cease to be valid and the quantum effects dominate. It is claimed that it is the smallest measurement of length with any meaning.* (A quantum effect is any phenomenon which cannot be fully explained by classical mechanics or laws of physics but it can sometimes be indirectly inferred. Quantum has been defined as a very small quantity of electro-magnetic energy.

Quantum physics postulates that particles can exist in two states). Quantum physics says that a very small particle of subatomic size can exist as wave and particle. This, of course, is a scientific truth well said but without the knowledge of subtlety of things. The statement of *Planck's length* may fully be accepted. Then, what is the space occupied by it? It must be virtually nil. It is said that a photon (of light) is massless and occupies nil space. Planck's length is much smaller than photon. It is said that for this size,1.6 × 10^{-35}m, time and space cease to be valid. But according to Thirumoolar, the size of Atman is still many more times (a million times) smaller than *Planck's length*. Now you can understand the nature of Atman. But can it be understandable?

The approximate size of Atman 'particle' as given by Thirumoolar is 5 × 10^{-38} millimeter and in terms of meter, it is 5 × 10^{-41}. I think that a particle of this size may lose the distinction between matter and energy or may act as both or as energy alone. Is it measurable or contaminable? We cannot even imagine this size because our imagination will abruptly stop once the invisible state is reached. Then, what is the space occupied by it, if at all, a particle? It should, virtually, be nil. How can there be any destruction for such an abstraction-like particle? There is nothing mightier than knowledge. Life is knowledge and is the mightiest and at the same time it is subtler than subtle.

Life actually signifies **the beingness of abstract intelligence in infinitesimal fraction**. (For convenience's sake, this infinitesimal fraction is referred to as Life 'particle' in this book) Abstraction denotes its unlimitedness. Intelligence implies self-luminosity. The inherence of self-luminosity infers its absolute freedom. Starting as an infinitesimal fraction of the whole (i.e., of Space or Absolute intelligence), it manifests as mind i.e., Self or Atman for the purpose of creation and identifies (because of three gunas imparted to mind) as this and that.

Eliminating this and that (i.e., the difference) pure knowledge will alone remain. It follows impure or defective or imperfect knowledge is of mind because of gunas.

It is enough to say here that the Life 'particles' in continuity fill the Space (which includes ether) and at the same time, in Atman state, it is the ultimate unit 'particle' for the creation of this universe. Therefore, Life (filling Space) is omnipresent.

It is quite natural and logical that whatever is made of fundamental unit particle (in insentient state) should ultimately be dismantled into its constituent fundamental unit particle (in sentient state) intact without losing its originality. So, when this universe (or universes) is dissolved, it will revert to its original state of extremely infinitesimal Life through Atman. What will remain will be the *endless dark empty Space* as in the beginning and so the world or universe created in the middle (as an interim state of Atman) is *maya*.

Atman is Omnipresent (Creation)

Life in the form of Atman, is the raw material i.e., the fundamental unit for the creation of whatever we see in this universe which includes the celestial bodies. Creation of the universe is, simply, by the creation of five gross or major elements namely the ether, the air, the fire, the water, and the earth. These five gross elements, actually, make up the bodies of all living beings. Then, what are these five gross elements made of? They are the different atoms of different elements that we study in chemistry i.e., the different elements mentioned in the periodic table. And these elements are made up of their respective atoms. But the atoms of different elements are invariably made principally of protons (positively charged), electrons (negatively charged), neutrons (carrying no charge), and some other particles considered to be of less importance. From the statements of great sages, it may be inferred that they, in turn, are made up of the ultimate Atman 'particles' involving some unknown steps (may be many more steps). When an atom is formed like this, two things namely **consciousness and light (or fire)** are effectively curtailed or even cut off to a very great extent by way of combination even at the stage of formation of subatomic particles. How it is accomplished can never be known. However, the curtailed light associated with heat can be known by the emission of light and heat energy when an atom (anything in atom state) is destroyed (i.e., an atom is actually converted into its constituent particles on destruction). Atom of any element can get destroyed (or dismantled) only into its constituent particles and they ultimately, at the dissolution of the universe, will become its constituent Life 'particles' through Atman. Life 'particles' will ever remain as indestructible and unchanging one.

In fact, there is no such insentient thing (because an absolute insentient thing, by itself, cannot exist or can it enter into any reaction?) and it is only the conscious Atman which becomes (by its Maya power - a power of curtailing) insentient-like by combination and we call it as insentient or inanimate thing. **It is the Atman with the guna Tamas in mixed or blended state, gets into the insentient state.** How the unchanging reality (sentient Life) expresses itself as the changing universe (insentient beings or things) without forfeiting its nature is a mystery. However, as an analogy or testimony, it may be said that different atoms forming molecules (or a compound) by combination completely forfeits their nature. But on dismantling the molecules, the atoms freed from molecules regain its original nature in full. For example, hydrogen and oxygen are gases and they, on combination, become water molecules with altogether a different nature. The water molecules, on dismantling, form again the hydrogen and oxygen atoms intact in gaseous state. This may serve as a simple example.

Yajnavalkya, a great sage, describes Atman as given in Brhadaranyaka Upanishad. He says to his wife, "*Worlds reject him who knows worlds to be different from Atman. The gods reject him who knows the gods to be different from Atman. Beings* (living and non-living beings) *reject him who knows beings different from Atman. All reject him who knows all* (such as sky, air, fire, water, earth, darkness, light, sun, moon, living beings etc.) *to be different from Atman*". Specifically, two examples may be given as follows:

He who dwells in the darkness but is within it, whom the darkness does not know, whose body is the darkness and who controls the darkness from within is the inner controller – your own self (i.e., Atman) *and immortal – (3:7:13)*

He who dwells in the light but is within it, whom the light does not know, whose body is light, and who controls the light from within is the inner controller – your own self and immortal – (3:7:14)

It is to be understood that Atman (in fact Life) takes a body using insentient food materials. In general, insentient things become the body for living beings. Even darkness and light are the bodies as revealed above in Brhadaranyaka

Upanishad. That is, the combined Atmans that form the insentient things become the body for the Atman in free state.

It will be worthwhile to state, at this juncture, what the great thinker **Thiruvalluvar** of Tamil Nadu in his **Thirukkural** has said.

He says, *"Knowledge is the perception of the true thing in whatever thing, of whatever kind it is"* or whatever be the thing and whatever its kind be, the knowledge is to find everything is made up of the true thing- (Thirukkural, Arathuppal – Song number 355). The true thing, (unbelievably minute and invisible) mentioned here, is called as **Meiporul** in Tamil language, the one that exists for ever or is eternal. Meiporul is nothing but Life.

Bhagavad Gita says, *"By what one sees, the one (true) thing (Sat or Life) in the different major elements (ether, air, fire, water, and earth) is termed as knowledge. This knowledge is Sattva"* or That by which one indestructible Being is seen in all beings, inseparate in the separated, know thou that knowledge as pure - (18:20).

Bhagavad Gita says about Life or Being as,

There is no existence for what does not exist (absolute insentient things). There is no non-existence for the being (the true Being or Life). The philosophy or the truth of these two has been realized or perceived by Jnanis (all knowledgeable persons)– Bhagavad Gita 2:16

Know that 'that' (the true Being or Sat or Life) is indestructible. There is no one who can cause destruction for the one which pervades the entire things (visible as well as invisible things) - Bhagavad Gita 2:17

From these statements, it may be inferred that all insentient things including the animated body of living beings are not true and they, just appear to be true (as they will disappear one day) and what is true is the ultimate sentient constituent in those insentient things. That true thing is Life. (Please note that Lord Krishna does not attach himself in these two verses (i.e., he did not say that "that indestructible is he") and he indicates it as something else **though 'it' has become 'he'**)

Thiruvalluvar in his Thirukkural 351 expresses, *"Inglorious birth ensues to him who, by delusion, sees the things as things which are not things (i.e., he sees everything as mere things which are not true)*". In other words, "*The individual who fails to see the true thing in untrue things, gets inglorious birth and the birth becomes a glorious one in which, the individual sees the true thing in untrue things*".

From the above statement of Tiruvalluvar, it may be inferred that it is only an illusion, to see the insentient things as mere things which actually comprise (or are made up of) something else (i.e., Atman).

Now, let us consider an example. If we cut out a small piece of wood from a big part of wood (not only wood but anything else existing in this world), we would find it to be a chip of it. It is so for an ordinary thinking person without good education. But for a thinking educated person, it is not a just a piece and he thinks that the piece is made up of atoms of different elements. This is a scientific thinking. And he, further, goes on thinking and finds that all atoms (in our example wood or even in genes of living being) are invariably made up of protons, electrons, neutrons and some other particles of less importance. Still, an inquisitive curious person refers related scientific facts and finds that these are also formed of what has been named as **'quark'**. With available highly sophisticated scientific instruments, scientists have come up to the point of quarks. Some scientists are of the opinion that even the quarks should have been made of some other unknown fundamental particle. Some scientists call **Higgs boson** (produced by the interaction between quark and gluon) as 'God's' particle. But the cosmos/universe must have been made only from a single unique particle. Hence, even at this point of discovery of Higgs boson and quarks, scientists are too far away from the ultimate Life particle which is subtle. Only from subtle state a physical entity can emerge. You can consider this as the law of Nature.

Spiritually great persons just skip all these steps and come to a stage that everything is God (Atman) without bothering about the intermediate stages in the creation of everything (visible or invisible) existing in the universe. But there were great saints such as Dattatreya (a spiritual leader who is said to be the incarnation of three gods namely Siva, Vishnu, and Bramma or just Vishnu) has said, *"Atmans are the ones that become the universe by combination or joining"*. Research at the level of Atman is never possible to present a scientific proof considering its infinitesimal fraction (or for convenience's sake, its size) and subtlety. This will be something like research on Life or boundless knowledge. I don't think we can do research on Life which is attribute-less.

It is to be inferred or known that there are *two states of Atman* – one is the (seemingly permanent) **finite state** and the other one is (permanent) **infinite state**. The finite state is the combined state of Atmans forming insentient beings or things (illumined or not illumined) influenced by time. (The reader should understand that the insentient things, which are always in a state of constant change, will go from one state to another state or even *vice versa*. This process will continue forever until dismantling into its constituents, Atmans and from Atmans to Life particles in the end.) The other state is the effulgent form of individual conscious Atman which transcends time. This infinite Atman is the one that takes up a body using insentient food materials obtained from the ultimate source of plants (or vegetation) to become a living being and make the world bustling with activities. Plants utilize the five major elements constituting the universe for their growth and yields (which may serve as food, medicine, etc.). Therefore, the human body is the *microcosm* and the universe is the *macrocosm*. (*As an approximate analogy, we can say the evolution of the universe from Atman may be likened to the development of human being from a single cell, zygote*) It means Atman needs insentient things (food materials) to get a visible and active physical body which comprises the five major elements namely ether, air, fire, water, and earth. Atman can exist without a physical body but the physical body cannot exist without the Atman. Both states of Atman (i.e., finite Atman in combination and infinite Atman in solitude) will ultimately become the infinite Life particles on dissolution of the universe. There is, according to **Chandogya Upanishad**, akasa (ether or space) inside man and outside him. Whatever exists must be within these and ultimately, they become identical to Sat or Being.

In which, one sees nothing else, hears nothing else, understands nothing else, that is the infinite. But that in which one sees something else, hears something else, understands something else, is the finite. That which is infinite, is alone immortal, and that which is finite, is mortal. – (Chandogya Upanishad 7:24:1)

Verily, for him alone, who sees thus, reflects thus, and understands thus, Prana (Life) springs from Atman, aspiration from Atman, memory from Atman, akasa (space) from Atman, fire from Atman, water from Atman, appearance and disappearance from Atman, food from Atman, strength from Atman, understanding from Atman, contemplation from Atman, intelligence from Atman, will from Atman, mind from Atman, speech from Atman, name from Atman, hymns from Atman, rites (acts) from Atman, all this from Atman alone.– (Chandogya Upanishad 7:26:1

The individual effulgent Atman expresses its consciousness through the medium of living beings and its light form can only be perceived by self- realized individuals.

The ultimate constituent of whatever exists in this universe (or universes), whether living or non-living, visible or invisible beings, are Life. Let us call Life as Brahman (or Almighty) as Vedas call it. Vedas of India says, only in one quarter (1/4th) of the Space filled by Life particles leaving no space unoccupied (as base), all the universes or galaxies have been created and suspended. **And, it is also self-creating or expanding the universe!**

As a spider spreads out and withdraws (its thread), as on the earth grow the herbs (and trees), and as from a living man issues out the hair (on the head and body), so out of the imperishable (Brahman) does the universe emerge here (in this phenomenal creation). – Mundaka Upanishad 1:1:7

Chandogya Upanishad says, **"In the beginning** (before the creation of the universe), **there was Being alone, one only, without a second"**. That is, being one is many and being many is one. That Being willed, **"May I become many, may I grow forth (expand)."** – (6:2:2 and 6:2:3)

Therefore, Atman is **omnipresent.**

Atman is Omnipotent

Before we proceed further, we must have no doubt that Life is knowledge with inherent implicit mind and Atman is Life with explicit mind. In Life, mind is inactive and is in obscurity state. In Atman, mind may exist without any action and at the same time, can seem to exist in subtle or physical bodies as a separate entity representing the actions of individual self. Hence, the words Life and Atman can be used interchangeably according to the context or sometimes used inappropriately.

Whether Atman moves? The answer is 'YES' as already mentioned because first of all, it moves from a living body leaving it dead and/or motionless. Even the Life residing in the body is a wonder. How? Considering the human body, it has nine (9) obvious holes such as the holes of two ears, two eyes, two nostrils, two genital holes, and anus. And apart from these, there are innumerable minute holes throughout the surface of the body. Compared even to these minute holes on the body, the size of the Life (or Atman) is so many million times smaller and hence it is dead easy to come out of the body but it remains stationary (or anchored) for a prescribed (life) period of time! What shall I say about its mercy? Is it not really a great, great, great wonder? Oh my God! What is your real nature? The Isa Upanishad says,

This self (Atman) *is one unmoving. It is faster than mind. Having preceded this mind, it is beyond the reach of the senses. Ever ready, it outstrips all that run (including light). By its mere presence, it enables the activities of living beings (and also* insentient things). - 4.

It moves, and it moves not. It is far, and it is near. It is within all this (the existing inanimate and animate beings of the universe) *and it is also outside all this* (filling the space outside all) - 5.

The Kada Upanishad says,

This Atman is atom of atom size (very minute and subtle). *Hence, it is not attainable by debate -* (1:2:8). That is, it is beyond any debate.

This Atman, sitting or lying down, can go anywhere – (1:2:20).

This Atman can go anywhere – (1:3:2)

Now let us consider about insentient or inanimate things. Insentient things, in general, are the five gross elements that constitute the universe. These five major elements namely the ether, the air, the fire, the water, and the earth were **first made in subtle forms** by the combination of Atmans with the mind impregnated with Tamas guna which in turn is blended with the other two gunas. Rendering of sentient into insentient nature itself, is *Maya*. Thus, *Maya* wields a special power that conceals the true thing (Atman). Maya itself is an aspect of knowledge. The subtle forms of the five gross elements are again mixed among themselves in definite proportion to yield the physical form of the five major elements.

Let us disregard the subtle form of five gross elements which is beyond our knowledge and consider only the physical form. The five gross elements comprise the different elements that we find in periodic table in chemistry or physics book. These elements are broadly classified or grouped into five gross elements called space (or ether), air, fire, water, and earth (each with distinct characteristics) by Vedas. Atman, at first, may form subatomic particles (rendering them insentient by its Maya power through the guna, Tamas) by combination with some unknown steps or in some unknown stages. These subatomic particles themselves have drastically different properties and functions. These subatomic particles by some intricate mechanism may produce the principal particles (of the atoms) such as protons, electrons, and neutrons and they, in turn, the stable electrically neutral particles called atoms. Scientists can explore only up to the level of subatomic particles with insentient nature and never at the level of sentient Atman. (It is said that subatomic particles are being formed continuously in the space). As the universe has evolved only from a single unit particle as believed by scientists, more than one unit particle independent of each other cannot constitute the universe. There must be only one fundamental particle which in great number and by combination constitutes the subatomic, atomic, and molecular particles which in turn, the universe and that fundamental unit particle is Atman.

Atoms of different elements may combine to give molecules whose properties are entirely different from the properties of its constituent particles. For example, hydrogen and oxygen are gases with their respective properties. But when they combine, they form the liquid called water which has entirely different properties. How is it possible? Even the way in which the protons, electrons, neutrons and any other particles are held together in an atom is also a wonder. Different atoms in different proportions form different molecules or compounds. These molecules often occur together to form bigger particles to be seen by naked eye. Simply saying, large groups of atoms or molecules in turn form the bulk of matter encountered in the universe.

The energy of a bigger solid particle, formed by association of atoms or molecules, seems to be lower when compared to the total energy of the individual atom's energies put together. The reason for this can be attributed to the presence of other atoms which diminish the expression of individual atom's full energy. That is the freedom to express the individual energy is restricted. This is so in the case of atoms. When an atom is destroyed or broken, it releases enormous energy. Binding up of atoms into a molecule reduces its energy release. Even the movement of subatomic particles (photons) is tremendous and this seems a great wonder.

In short, the energy or strength for a bigger sized one is greater than the energy of individual particle due to combination/association of smaller particles. As the freedom of expression of energy by individual particle is restricted by the presence of other particles, the energy expressed by the bigger particle is less than the energy of individual particles put together. It may be said that **a very large amount of energy is locked up inside each discrete particle** but expression is restricted. I wish to caution that there may be some other reasons. It is beyond our knowledge to reveal all the reasons associated. But what is true is that as the particle size goes below the size of subatomic sizes, it exhibits unusual properties. **Hence, the ultimate particle Atman** (active form of life) **is omnipotent**. The word omnipotent is also applicable to its ability to become the numerous diversified beings (both sentient and insentient beings seen in this world). Thus, unity is not different from diversity. One reality alone shines forth as both. In other words, Life alone shines forth as sentient and insentient beings of the universe.

That Being which is this subtle essence (cause), even that all this world has for its self. That is the true. That is the Atman– (Chandogya Upanishad 6:8:7)

Even in the case of living beings, smaller sized living beings in great number seem to be more powerful than bigger sized living being. For example, bacteria in greater number can kill a human being or even an elephant. Virus which is many times smaller than bacterium is more powerful than a bacterium.

Now, let us consider about the celestial bodies and earth suspended in the space. These celestial bodies (especially planets) **have some subtle control over the earth** (as well as with each other) **as well as on the terrestrial lives and the lives within the water, sea and space, though they are inanimate things.** How do they control is a mystery or beyond our knowledge? Therefore, considering the above points, Atman is **omnipotent**.

Atman is Omniscient

There exist only two beings – sentient (living) and insentient (non-living) beings or those which are with conscious and those which are with almost nil consciousness. The only thing with consciousness is individual Atman and all other things (combined Atmans) in the universe are without consciousness. However, those without consciousness can exhibit their potentialities if intelligently used (computers, smart phones). Thus, some insentient things (such as silicon) are bestowed with wonderful and unbelievable properties that will leave you astonished. Scientists are making the insentient things *sensible* (**not knowledgeable**) to the extent possible (for example robots etc.). As an analogy, through inappropriate, we can say that current is to inanimate machines as Life is to living beings.

In living beings, Life animates the insentient things (cells in the organs of the body) and makes them vibrant. A person with some education in biochemistry knows to a considerable extent the wonderful works of various organs of the body and about the magical works of hormones and enzymes within the body.

Now, let us again turn to a human body with Life and a human body without Life. A person bustling around with Life can see, hear, taste, speak, smell, and feel the touch with the help of respective parts in the body. And he can think; he can enjoy with his senses and at the same time suffer from them also. You can include whatever the human beings can think and do. In short, he has knowledge i.e., Life. But his knowledge is restricted by his karma, a powerful subtle tool created by the free-willed individual himself. Even with this restricted knowledge, humans have invented and/or discovered so many scientific wonders which are being enjoyed by common people. Though the human being is a repository of inestimable potentialities, he is able, however, to use them only to an insignificant extent because of karma.

In fact, great fundamental inventions are made only through intuitions (or instincts). Based on fundamental inventions, numerous modifications and improvements, tapping the uses, have come up. How all these are possible? Whether a dead body can do all these things? Whether it has any potential? Can you imagine anything which, without Atman (i.e., Life), can do this?

Consider the plant kingdom. What a wonderful and fascinating creation. Whether the plants can produce conspicuous, variously and wonderfully colored flowers and fruits of various types with enchanting tastes, without the Life within them. The wonders of living beings are only due to the presence of Life in them. All types of products (including drugs) that we get from plant kingdom is inexhaustible. We cannot put in words the magic performed by Life in various living beings and even by insentient things. Copying the nature, the scientists are doing wonders of many kinds.

You take all branches of science and all branches of arts including music, sports, etc., how the human beings are excelling in them? You may say it may be due to brain work. **Whether the brain will work in the absence of Atman?** Brain can act only as a medium but it cannot be a source of knowledge. It is Atman that is the source of knowledge. But alas! Knowledge is restricted as already mentioned and that too to various degrees in accordance with the karma earned so far.

First of all, we must understand that knowledge is something in humans that has to be tapped or grown with education. What is education? Education is the exploration and research on Nature (both living and non-living beings) putting questions such as how, why, and what and getting answers. Research is a type of thinking and experimentation with the help of existing facts or available data and instruments to some fruition. Education is, simply, probing and understanding the Nature.

Humans effectively copy the Nature. The initial requirement for research is the thinking based on need and bringing it into reality. Just thinking and putting questions themselves improve knowledge.

Scientists are also involved in search of the ultimate unit particle. Why are they involved in search of the ultimate particle? Because they have come to know that ultimate unit particle is the one that has blossomed into this universe. Scientists think it to be **something else** other than the particles known so far *not knowing that the ultimate fundamental unit particle is right within them as Atman.* **What a funny situation it is!** Is it possible to catch hold of Atman and do research on it?

Now, we know with some simple reasoning that Atman is omnipresent, omnipotent, and omniscient because Life is omnipresent, omnipotent, and omniscient. Life is named, in Vedas, as Brahman which means one who is all surpassing great or vast and unlimited or simply Almighty. Let us look at the definition of Brahman. It is defined as **"Existence, Knowledge, and Bliss"**. What a great and wonderful definition it is! It is Existence as there is nothing but this. It is knowledge since it is omniscient and hence omnipotent. That knowledge is inexhaustible, invincible, infinite, incorruptible and ever present. Because of its knowledge, it is Bliss. Therefore, Life or Brahman is knowledge full of Bliss and it is **omniscient.**

Brahman (The supreme reality is existence, knowledge and bliss) - Vedas – Hinduism.

Yayweh (He brings into existence whatever exists) – Bible – Christianity.

Allah (The one and only one God) – Quran -Islam.

To put together, the supreme reality (which is existence, knowledge, and bliss) is the only one God that brings into existence or becomes whatever exists.

Gods

Brahman thought, "I have created the universe; now, I shall create the governors (rulers or gods)". (Birhadaranyaka Upanishad)

Brahman created the gods better than he. Inasmuch as being himself as mortal, he created immortals. Therefore, this is a surpassing creation. (Birihadaranyaka Upanishad1:4:5)

*They say to worship this god and that god. But **all gods are many appearances of Brahman**.* (Brihadaranyaka Upanishad 1:4:5)

In the beginning, the Atman knew he is Brahman. Therefore, it (Atman) became everything. And whosoever among gods realized, it became Brahman. It was similarly so among the sages and men. (Brihadaranyaka Upanishad 1:4:10)

The above four statements in the Upanishad are to be deeply thought of. The first passage means that Brahman itself (becoming inactive or concealing the consciousness) became the universe which exclusively refers to insentient ones. Then, it thinks of creation of gods. The second passage says that in order to rule over the universe, he created **active** gods with immortality being himself **inactive** (i.e., being witness in living beings and being insentient things of the universe i.e., as mortal). That is, Brahman's part is to become everything and the gods part is to rule and control. Vedas state the creation of gods as a surpassing creation. It is a surpassing creation because it is superior to other creations. Why is it superior? This creation is superior because gods are meant to rule over the universe or universes. Who are those gods? Third passage gives the answer that gods are none but Brahman in various forms. That is, they are **none but the images of Brahman**. The fourth passage says that Atman knew that he is Brahaman **in the beginning** (i.e., when first created) and as a consequence, he became everything i.e., he found himself to be the whole universe. Who can become Brahman or identify himself with the whole universe? Anybody, be it gods, sages, or ordinary human beings, says the fourth passage, can become Brahman provided the individual **realizes** himself as Brahman. What remains to be answered is, "How to realize oneself as Brahman?" First, he (i.e., an ordinary human being) should realize himself as Isvara, the first God created. How to realize oneself as Isvara? It is by purifying the mind or by getting back the absolute mind. How to purify the mind? It is by not becoming subservient to mind without yielding to all types of desires and thus getting rid of karma. By becoming Isvara with purification of mind, he becomes all knowledgeable with no question lingering in him. And he, ultimately, becomes Brahman. That is, he becomes Brahman through Isvara's stage. Isvara is also called as the **first guru** (teacher) to guide others to attain salvation.

Becoming of God, Isvara

When Poornar or Poornam (a perfect complete embodiment of Brahman or Life in Atman state) reflected through Maya (a mind with absolute pure Sattva guna), it became Isvara. Shiva is considered as Isvara in Hinduism.

[This Maya has with it the mixed gunas namely Sattva in Sattva, Rajas in Sattva, and Tamas in Sattva. When Isvara reflected through the mind of Sattva in Sattva guna, he became Vishnu. That is why Vishnu (God of protection and also of water) is often called as Isvara. Vishnu is also depicted as mind or Mayavan. When Isvara reflected through Rajas in Sattva guna, he became Brahma or Prajapati (God of creation of living beings and also of earth) and as Brahma came after Vishnu in continuation, Brahma is said to be born of Vishnu. When Isvara reflected through the guna, Tamas in Sattva, he became Rudra (the God of destruction and also of fire). As Rudra came after Brahma in continuation, Rudra is said to be born of Brahma. In short, these are the different forms of Isvara. Isvara or Shiva is also called as Mahadeva (God of air) and Sadhashiva (God of space or ether)]

Shiva *tattva* (principle) is to live by renunciation of everything to attain spiritual enlightenment in the end.

Vishnu *tattva* (principle) is to enjoy anything with detachment and attain spiritual enlightenment in the end.

Both the *tattvas* (principles) involve discarding of three bodies namely gross, subtle and causal bodies at the time of enlightenment.

Isvara is said to be the master of mind or *Maya*. (The capital letter 'G' is applied in this book only for God Isvara) He is of light form. Atman is the subtle form for him. Therefore, **Atman is Isvara.** God that we are worshiping is the first God Isvara (direct from Poornar or Satchithanandar). Isvara is often referred to as Self (Self of selves) and the other Atmans are referred to as selves.

God takes different names as **Isvara to Hindus, as Father (whom Jesus referred to as, "I am in Him; He is in me") to Christians, and Allah to Muslims.**

Let us see what the Upanishads say about God Isvara.

Mandukya Upanishad: *This is the Lord of all – their knower, their inner controller, their source, their origin and dissolution.* (6)

Munndaka Upanishad: *The Purusha is transcendental, since he is formless. And since he is coexistence with all that is external and internal and since he is birthless, therefore he is without vital force and without mind* (because he exists in Atman state with dormant or inactive mind i.e., a mind without desires or with Sattva guna); *he is pure and superior to the (other) superior imperishable (gods) – (2: I:2)*

From him (Isvara) originates the vital force as well as the mind, all the senses, space, air, fire, water, and earth that supports all (2:1:3)

Isavasya Upanishad: *He, the Self-existent* **without a body***, is everywhere - without muscles, and without the taint of sin; radiant, whole, and* *pure; seeing all, knowing all. He duly assigns their respective duties for eternal gods. – (8)*

Svetasvatra Upanishad: *The person (or Purusha) is, indeed, the great Lord; he is the impeller of internal organs towards the absolute pure attainment. He is the ruler, the light, and the indestructible.*

Brihadaranyaka Upanishad: *God has two states or forms- gross and subtle. Gross state is destructible, bounded, and knowable or defined. The subtle state is indestructible, not bounded, and unknowable or undefined. (2:3:1)*

Patanjali: Patanjali, a great sage, has said that *"Isvara is a special creation who is untouched by grief, acts and their benefits, desires, etc."*

God can be without form or with subtle form and he may take a physical form for his ardent devotee. God is simply omnipresent, omnipotent, and omniscient. No law can bind him. He is the sole controller of the created universe. He has no form but can take any form. The eight great (Sattva guna attributes) attributes of God Isvara are:

1. Peerless (self-conscious as Brahman)

2. Always in pure form (subtle or in between subtle and physical i.e., fire form)

3. Natural sensed (omnipresence)

4. Omniscience (all knowledgeable)

5. By nature, bondless (naturally with no attachment of any kind)

6. Limitless grace (showing boundless kindness and mercy)

7. Omnipotent (all-powerfulness)

8. Boundlessly blissful

Isvara, being bodiless Atman, is God and he is immortal. The first incarnation (not by birth but directly) of Brahman/Life in the form of Atman with the above eight attributes is Isvara. As Isvara is with mind in Suguna Brahman state, he is called as *Ardhanaisvara*.

God (Isvara or Self) is the sole ruler and controller of all other Atmans with karma (or souls or selves with karma) **and the universe. He is the God of gods. Him, we are worshipping as God.**

I want to quote at this stage, what a great devotee by name Manikkavasagar (one of four Nayanmars) has said about Shiva(n) in his 'Thiruvasagam'. Thiruvasagam is considered as the essence of Vedas without any ambiguity. Manikkavasagar considered Shiva, the Isvara or Isa, as Brahman (*in Atman state*) itself. He worshipped Isvara in both sugana Brahman and nirguna Brahman states. I give, here, only the meaning of Tamil version in the form of songs given in 'Kovil Thiruppathigam' of 'Thiruvasagam'.

I present here the translation only for the important part of each song (not for full song) in 'Kovil Thiruppathigam'. The meaning which I give here is only a speck of the vast meaning.

Oh! The one that appears as great bright light within me, be graceful to allow me, by plugging all the ways of five senses, to see the true nature of your being.

You, (Shivaperuman or just Shiva), being the origin and pervading the whole universe are the endless first one.

You remain the one to be perceived by the one who has surrendered the soul and body. You just dissolve those (such as body) which stand as false darkness. You grace me with the power to perceive or know the way to say about you.

You are peerless. You are the Life of all lives. You being the distinct pure Space as pitch darkness, emerged from that pitch darkness as pure bright space (or light). You are guna-less (without the three gunas) *bliss.*

You are defect-less whole (full) *or perfect. You are the hill of illuminating flame without end. You are the stabilized one in mind. You have my body as your abode. What can I ask you?*

You became the gross or physical forms of space, air, fire, water, and earth constituting the whole universe and at the same time, you concealed yourself (in subtle form) *in them as if you are not the space, air, fire, water, and earth. This, I enjoyed by recognizing you in them.*

I thought you without forgetting that there is nothing else apart from you i.e., you are everything (in the universe). *That everything, then, by successive dismantling gets into atomic state first and then by further successive disintegration will become the ultimate fundamental one* (as before the creation of the universe). *That ultimate fundamental one is you. Thus, I came to know that there is no single thing* (in the universe) *that is not you* (i.e., there is nothing apart from you or you are everything).

Who is able to know you (by this way? Oh, you remain unfathomable!

Oh! The pervading bright light! You are the one growing into everything and pervading the vast boundless universe (or Space). Who is my relative or is there anyone who is not my relative in this world? i.e., all are my kith and kin or images of you. Oh! My light, you make me blissful.

You appear (as this universe) in fire form, being a formless one. Nobody can say about your origin, interim state (becoming the universe) and your end state. You sever the bondage with this world. You are the endless bliss.

I got the endless bliss from you. What have you got from me? I don't have anything to give to you in return.

In Thiruvarthai of Thiruvasagam he says, in Song – 1, that *whoever knows the grace of God (Isvara) of coming down on earth in the mantle of human being to reveal the primal source, Brahman, becomes my Lord.* It means, "One becomes Brahman through the grace of Isvara or simply God".

The **most important concept of Hinduism** is that Brahman expresses itself as **nirguna**

Brahman (Atman without form) as well as **saguna Brahman (Atman with human form or any living being form).** Nirguna Brahman is without gunas or not influenced by gunas (or qualities). Saguna Brahman is with the taintless eight gunas all related to Sattva guna. ***Brahman needs to be with gunas** (i.e., Saguna Brahman or Isvara) **in order to rule and control the universe or universes*** and being in Sattva guna, he just acts as a pure judge with compassion. Isvara is considered as **both nirguna Brahman** *(without form)* **and saguna Brahman** *(with form or body)* in Hinduism.

A human being is not a pure unisexual (biologically). Each human organism bears the potentialities of both male and female sex. It is the predominance of one over the other sex that determines the sexuality. Masculinity and femininity are not mutually exclusive and so, the possibility of intermediate sex exists.

Isvara, as already said, is also termed as Ardha-narisvara. The name Ardhanarisvara is a combination of words, *ardha, nari, and isvara* meaning *half, woman,* and isvara *(male or purusha)* respectively. God is Isvara (Purusha or knowledge) and woman part is Shakti or *maya* or mind. Shakti is considered to be the consort (wife) of Isvara.

The fusion of Shiva and shakti into Ardhanarisvara representing the male and female halves (or the knowledge and mind), transcends the distinction between and limitation of male (knowledge) and female (mind). This fusion takes Isvara beyond gender manifest. That is why Isvara is worshipped in the form of Linga which shows the combination of knowledge and mind symbolizing the union of male and female principles (or even sex organs). It also depicts the formless form (invisible form) of Shiva or Atman.

Realization of Brahman as knowledge leads to liberation. That is, taking in of mind within knowledge (union of knowledge and mind) leads to liberation or it may also be inferred that if the inner masculine (Life/knowledge) and feminine (mind) meet or merge, the individual will be in a perpetual state of ecstasy. (This happens in deep sleep state also but unconsciously). When the individual does it (or copulates) with a woman (outside), it becomes transitory and all troubles that come with it, are an ongoing drama. Even in copulation with opposite sex (i.e., a woman with a man or a man with a woman), *the real ecstasy or rapturous state is exclusively felt within the individual only* and it does not flow from the opposite sex. That is why masturbation sends the individual (male or female) into a rapturous state. This accounts for homosexuality also.

Sex is not a sin provided it is meant to develop inter-relationship with opposite sex and to populate by giving birth to offspring along with pure love to be transformed into universal love in a society. (*Sex does not seem to be influenced by religion, caste, or sect and can break any barrier, even the human or physical barrier. Frankly speaking, sex does know not the differences*) **As we are all descendants of a single source, we must all be invariably related to one another.** Therefore, religion must be treated as a human made for difference's sake. **Religion has nothing to do with God.** Caste and sect are deliberately introduced by ego-afflicted humans.

Human beings are, in fact, **self-degenerated descendants of God** (Ardhanarisvara) by virtue of acquiring more and more *ahamkara* (ego) and detachment from oneness with identity or individuality coupled with added karma. This **descendancy** of living beings, not being exclusively unisexual from Shiva in Ardhanarisvara form, seems to be meaningful as well as viable. **Degeneration** can be known from the gradual decline taking place through the four yugas (world periods) namely *Krita yuga, Treta yuga, Dwapara yuga, and Kali yuga.* The current yuga or the world period is Kali yuga.

Krita yuga: It is the age of truth with godliness and divine qualities. Dharma is believed to stand on four legs. Dharma is said to constitute the qualities – *patience, forgiveness, piety, self-control, honesty, sanctity, control of senses, reason, knowledge or vidya, and truthfulness.* Added to dharma is ahimsa which is benevolence or love or goodwill or tolerance or all the above. It is characterized by Sattva guna.

Treta yuga: It is the age of virtue and wisdom. In this yuga, dharma is said to stand on three legs. Sattva guna is predominant over other gunas.

Dwapara yuga: Predominant guna is Rajas over other gunas. Dharma is said to stand on two legs.

Kali yuga: This yuga is dominated by Tamas over other gunas. Dharma is said to stand on one leg.

For the sake of briefness, it is just enough to know that there was general decline of dharma, ahimsa, wisdom, knowledge, and even life-span in the succeeding yugas. Until the Dwapara yuga, human beings were excessively more dependent on gods for their powers than their own powers based on bodily strength and acquired knowledge. In this respect also, it has been gradual.

Let us not concentrate on or consider the other three yugas but on the Kali yuga. Scientifically thinking, the beginning of Kali yuga was different since the knowledge was almost reduced to animals. Kali yuga must have preceded by a long period after a great natural calamity leaving only those at remote and obscure places. Even today, there are people at remote and obscure places having meagre knowledge and living like animals. Now you can understand what will be left over if at all a full-fledged nuclear war ensues.

In the beginning of Kali yuga, many of the prosimian species as well as anthropoid's species created would have gone extinct. New species would have come up. Appearance and disappearance would have occurred in accordance with the changes, challenges, catastrophes and the need of the time. Evolution do not have any part to play but only the challenges and necessities bring about all the changes and that too within some limits. Monkey will ever remain as monkey and it applies to all. I think evolution theory has been given undue importance.

In the beginning, humans, whose physical make- up depended/depends on environment (geographical placement) and the way of life, lived like animals. Gradually, they grew in knowledge by observing the Nature. Initially what dominated were sex and protection against adverse conditions and predators with migration, accommodating themselves to new places. Then, power and comfort became the goals. Humans were destined to gain knowledge only by observing the Nature. Even today, it is so. In due course of time, spirituality was first to come up only to be overshadowed by materialistic life with more and more advance in scientific knowledge (copying the Nature and using it advantageously is the scientific knowledge). With the advancement of scientific knowledge, power and self-protection have assumed the top priority and for this purpose, hypocrisy has become the powerful surreptitious weapon. Truth will sustain. Spirituality can never be erased and Nature will have the last laugh. Nature is not different from God.

Human being became more and more separated from oneness state as he false-identified in due course of time (or in successive yugas) as separate identity relying more and more on his growth of self-knowledge and power. He has started to think that whatever the knowledge and power he has are of his own and not of God.

In the beginning, this (universe) was but the self of a human form. He reflected and found nothing else but himself. (That is, the self or Atman got a human form) *He first uttered, "I am he (Brahman)". Therefore, he was called 'Aham'. Hence, to this day, when a person is addressed, he first says, "It is I", and then says the other name (i.e., his proper name) that he may have.* – Brahadaranyaka Upanishad 1:4:1

He was not at all happy. Therefore, people (still) are not happy when alone. He desired a mate. He became as big as man and wife embracing each other. He parted his very body into two. From that came husband and wife (a separate identity for mind). Therefore, said Yajnavalkya, this body is one-half of oneself, like one half of the two halves of a split pea. Therefore, this space is indeed filled by the wife. He was united with her. From that, men (humans) *were born.* - Brahadaranyaka Upanishad 1:4:3

A split without losing its wholeness. That is, the space left by one half is filled by the wife (in suppressed state) with respect to male. And with respect to female, one half is filled by the husband (in suppressed state). That is, either the male or female is not a pure unisexual. This statement by Yajnavalkya was included to indicate that the male or female is not a pure unisexual. In addition, there is an intermediate state also.]

She thought, "How can he be united with me after producing me from himself". Well, let me hide myself. She became a cow, the other became a bull and was united with her; from that, cows were born. The one became a mare, the other a stallion; the one became a she-ass the other became a he-ass; and was united with her; from that one-hoofed animals were born. The one became a she-goat, the other one became a he-goat; the one became a owe, the other became a ram and was united with her; from that, goat and sheep were born. Thus, did he project everything that exists in pair, down to the ants. - Brahadaranyaka Upanishad 1:4:4.

(The above statement of Brahadaranyaka Upanishad 1:4:4 serves as an example and it includes each and every living beings)

Isvara himself or in the form of Vishnu or Brahma is termed as *Hiranyagrabha* meaning the universal womb/egg or golden womb/egg. Devotees refer Atman as the first seed for the creation of the universe. The same concept is wonderfully depicted in the installation of the idol of main deity in a very small room rightly called *karuvarai* (womb-room) or *moolasthanam* (place of origin) or *grabhgriha* (sanctum sanctorum) in a big Hindu temple in India. We must try to understand that the other installations in Hindu temples are all symbolic.

Evolution of Mind

Mind is the carrier of karma earned by mind itself, speech, and body. Initially, when an Atman was provided with a body, the mind would have been in pure state. This pure pristine state is the absolute condition. In absolute condition of mind, the Atman is said to be conscious of its source i.e., Isvara and so the individual knew him as Brahman. In due course of time, the mind assuming the freewill or freedom strengthens itself with egoism and enters into 'I' ness or thinks itself a separate entity (as a son to his father). The individual, then engaging himself into good or bad activities or both, earns karma and acquires a relative mind with obvious showing up of gunas. This relative mind confers the individual with identification. Thus, the basic difference or identification among individuals lies in the mental constitution.

An individual, who is determined in knowing the Reality (Brahman) should know *the worlds are acquired through karma. There is nothing* (here in this world) *that is not the result of karma* - Mundaka Upanishad 1:2:11

Departing successively from absolute condition of mind with each and every rebirth, the individual's relative mind absorbs the essence of thoughts and activities experienced in those births as qualities and impressions (*vasanas*). This absorption of *vasanas* by relative mind with each and every birth is termed as continuity of mind. By this way, the mind gets more and more into relative condition drifting away from the initial absolute condition i.e., from the conscious of Isvara state.

This relative condition of mind involved in the relish of worldly pleasures ensures the Atman further births to enjoy the worldly pleasures through the five senses (ear, eyes, nose, tongue, and skin). Relative mind acquired actually serves as the real identification for each and every soul.

When the individual takes a fresh birth, he gets a relative mind from the very first birth. However, when gods take birth, they get back to the original state after each and every birth. Usually, they take birth on an errand. Even if they commit any unethical act or adultery, they repent or get punishment immediately. At the end of punishment, they get back to their original state.

In general, the relative mind obtained from the previous births is termed as chitta or chittam. The chittam becomes the inner subconscious mind in a conditioned and condensed state. Chittam is only a store house. (It is the knowledge (with absolute pure mind) that is responsible for the intuition or instincts. Intuition never goes wrong). The contents of the inner mind (chittam) will be the impressions of knowledge gained or lost from all sorts of righteous and unrighteous acts with what has been experienced of them.

This happens in each successive birth. If, in the previous birth, the individual happened to be an intelligent or learned, it may become an innate quality for him in the next or present birth. Such innate quality may consistently be apparent in the next birth as enhanced intelligent. That is, it will be carried over to the next birth. There may be ups and downs in accordance with the changes in karma. The changes may be based on good and bad karmas. This applies not only for intelligence but also for other aspects such as foolishness, skills in speech, music, education, memory power, understanding power, sports, etc., etc. That is why we see different grades in intelligence or skills. We see some individuals are born with some inherent knowledge, skill, and ability and some others are not. Thus, the extraordinary powers of prodigies are not due to heredity or environment or by the interaction of the two (heredity and environment) but due to karma. Earning karma may depend on environment. This is one aspect of karma.

The other aspect of karma decides what, how, and where one's birth will be, what will be the next birth, what will be the status of life, what will be the physical state, and what will be the disease state? Thus, the overall nature or buildup of the individual is solely based on his karma earned by him. Even the degree of performance of any individual's brain and its sharpness are dependent on karma earned. Thus, the inequality in a genius or a moron is due to karma and not due to heredity or environment because heredity and environment themselves are the result of karma. In my opinion, nothing can occur by chance. Even luck is based on karma.

Mainly karma refers to merits or virtue (punya) and demerits or vice (sins). The merits are acquired through righteous acts and good characters. The demerits are acquired through unrighteous acts and bad characters.

Each soul would have passed innumerable births and deaths in each world period or yuga. Many world periods would have passed. Births would also have been innumerable from single celled or single sensed living beings to six sensed living being. By meditation, one can awaken the memories of his past lives. That means, what is *subtly* stored in mind can be retrieved. As a result of the perception of subliminal impressions, one may gain the knowledge of all his former lives. Buddha is said to have gained the knowledge of all his former lives. Even some devotees are said to have gained memories of their former lives.

In each world period (or yuga), many souls would have attained liberation from births and deaths. This could be a continuous process.

The outer exhibited mind of the individual in the fresh or latest birth is thus actually based on the impressions or dispositions (*vasanas*) gained in the inner mind chittam from so many previous births. Hence, his acts and thoughts will be in conformity with them. His overall character, behavioral pattern and personality also depend on it. The mind with karma becomes the cause even for the very next birth along with unfulfilled desires which shape his reincarnation. Thus, chitta we have got now would be of numerous births old or countless years old. Simply saying, the present relative mind is the conglomeration of all the minds of previous births. Verily, no two minds are exactly identical with each other.

It is really amazing that **Life seems to entrust all the activities to mind and whatever the enjoyments** (such as pleasure) **or sufferings** (such as pain) **or any adverse effects of the acts**

ensuing, it takes up only through the mind and its soldiers (the five senses). Thus, Life seems to rejoice or suffer temporarily through mind. However, Life in Atman seems to caution the mind by intuition on the activities of mind especially of bad activities. Whenever the mind ignores such cautions, the individual is in a fix (or trouble).

It is *ahamkara* (ego) or mind born out of separate entity (as a son feels independent of his father) that is responsible for all difficulties and dissatisfactions. *Ahamkara is ignorance. Ahamkara* or ego springs up immediately from the first birth itself. It compels one into action earning karma. When it gets strengthened, birth ensues. It is a cognitive error evidenced in the mind's intelligence as a result of separate entity. This error transforms itself into ignorance.

As we are provided with freewill to earn karma, so are we provided with freewill to do away with karma. When all the acts and thoughts are disowned completely, the mind gets purified, bodily desires vanish and the *ahamkara* or ego is won. As a result, the relative mind gets (chitta or chittum) back to its pure absolute mind. This pure absolute mind is termed as **sattvam**. When you become impersonal with your body, you become personal with Atman (or God) in you. The great siddhar, Kagapusundar, says **this** (absolute) **mind will, then, become the Life itself** i.e., Brahman itself.

Just as a bird tied to a string, after flying in various directions and finding no resting place elsewhere, takes refuge at the very place where to it is tied, even so, dear boy, that mind, after flying in various directions and finding no resting place elsewhere, takes refuge in Prana (Life) alone; for the mind, dear boy, is tied to Prana. – Chandogya Upanishad 6:8:2

When the individual's mind dissolves and becomes Life (Brahman) itself, it is a**dvaitam**. When the mind remains with no karmic acts, the individual becomes all-knowing and Brahman alone remains the supreme reality, it is **vishishtadvaitam**. This is the state usually obtained by great devotees and Jnanis (persons with wisdom). They can take birth as they wish but they will not get bounded by karma because they disown the benefits of karma. Jesus Christ can be cited as an example. If at all karma results, they have to nullify the karma by repentance or suffering or by taking birth. God just acts as a true judge with no partiality.

Human Body

A layman or an ordinary person may know that he has Life, mind, and body. Even among them, many may not be aware of or uncared of them.

Essentially, a human being is endowed with Life, mind, and a body. An ordinary person may just know about waking state, dream state, and sleep state but he may not know that these three states are different with different functions and significances and they have something to tell him.

Before we proceed to know about the three states, it is better to know that we have three bodies namely physical (or gross), subtle, and casual bodies corresponding to the three states and of these only a few are aware. In waking state, all the three bodies are active. In dream state, subtle and casual body are active and in deep sleep state only, the casual body is active.

For understanding purpose, we may say that, in waking state, Atman (Life and mind) and body are in a conscious state. In dream state, the Life being luminous acts as a spectator; and the mind, getting detached, becomes active creating its own world. In (dreamless) sleep state, Atman

(Life with dormant mind) alone is conscious enjoying the bliss.

In waking state, we think and engage ourselves in all types of activities with our physical body. When you are involved in imagination, you are actually with your subtle body and you can also be in association with your beloved one at a far-off place with subtle body in imagination. In deep meditating state, forgetting the outside world and even your body you are in causal body.

In dream state, the mind creates its own world and enjoys with the physical body but in a subtle state i.e., a body without substance. Dreaming is true and that we have a body in dream state is also true. From this, we can come to a conclusion that we do have a subtle body. Hence, the subtle body needs no proof for its existence. It actually exists. This is the body a human can have after death. Sometimes, the individual with the subtle body becomes a ghost as a result of mental make-up in present birth after death. This subtle body is ghost body. This ghost body, which can superimpose on a living person's body, has a greater influence. After possessing a living person, the ghost can show all its violent behaviors and acts intermittently or occasionally. Often times, it may remain calm without affecting the person possessed or leave his body suddenly. Simply saying, a person may get possessed by ghost. From this, it can be derived that inanimate things can have subtlety. Human body itself is made up of inanimate things. (Because, the five major elements are first created in subtle forms and then the subtle forms are mixed to arrive at physical forms of the five major elements.)

The other body is the casual body which cannot be seen. In causal body that is in dreamless deep sleep, the mind is reposing in Life without any activities. Thinking stops and hence, the person, who was in deep sleep, on waking does not know what he experienced in deep sleep state. To be exact, the **casual body is Atman itself with ignorance** (because of ego and karma) but for the sake of keeping the body alive, it causes the involuntary functions to continue including the breathing process. But on waking, the individual can come to know that he had a good peaceful and joyous sleep. Moreover, his physical body will also be fresh and active with renewed energy on waking. We must note that we experience only the bliss in deep sleep state and not the mixed happiness, unhappiness, fear, pain and such all as in dream or waking states.

In dream state, the mind creates its own world of incoherence. Everything will be in a haphazard incoherent manner and the experiences in dream world will also be in haphazard manner. Often it is incoherent and weird. This indicates mind is not having its own knowledge and it gets knowledge from Life and that too is hazy as the moon-light which is the light got from sun. (We know that things will not be clear under moon-light). Mind is not self-luminous but it basks in the luminosity of Life. Thus, the light we get in dream state is only from Life. The only source of light for the world in dream is Life often mentioned as Atman. When we get vivid memories of dream, we must know that Life/Atman being a spectator also takes part partially.

(Dreams interspersed with fears are the result of fears experienced in waking state and also due to imagination and real fear in difficult situations such as catastrophes in various previous births including the present birth. Dreams are not due to brain or changes in brain chemicals as suggested by scientists or doctors. It is purely of mind's work. Some drugs may produce nightmares in sleep state. Such dreams are mainly due to disturbances in the brain which affect the confused normal dream which itself is frightening. Dreams are often impressions of death-fears experienced in various births including births of animals, birds, etc. Brain cannot carry the impressions of previous births because it forms only a part of the (dead) body. It is the mind that carries the impressions of previous births. Hence, it is verily the act of mind and not that of brain).

Another thing is about dreaming in black and white or in color. All dreams are mostly or essentially in black and white. If it is said to be in color, it must be a cognitive error or impression biased. We dream under the effulgence of Atman. This effulgence of Atman is without the three gunas and hence, the light is pure white (and black) without colors. Whereas the light, we get in waking state, is dubbed with three gunas and hence we see colors. That means the **light of Atman is entirely different from the light we get from insentient things (including the sun) in the universe** which is dubbed with colors as a result of the infusion of three gunas. One more thing is what we get as compulsion physically is reflected subtly in dreams. For example, if your urinary bladder is full with urine, you get the feeling of pissing but not actually pissing. The dream we get in this condition will be somewhat frustrating and inconvenient. This compulsion will make you wake. On waking, we immediately go for urinating or for emptying the bowels and get a great relief.)

In waking state, the mind is active in association with sense organs such as ears, eyes, nose, tongue and skin. In dream state also the mind is active with sense organs but in subtle forms. That means we hear, feel the tough, see, taste, and smell even with subtle organs. In deep sleep state, the mind is reposing temporarily in Life.

In waking state, whatever the individual does is only in association with mind which, in turn, is in association with sense organs. He enjoys the benefits of action (good or bad). When a good act is done by sharing or by disowning the benefit, it accumulates as merit or virtue (punya) to him. When a bad act, which inflicts dissatisfaction or pain or any adverse effect on others, is done, it ends in demerit or sin to him. These merits and demerits will have a snow-ball effect ending in fate (a mixture of good and bad fate) or *kanmam* or simply karma. Here, he does own the benefits of his actions and thoughts **consciously**.

In contrast to waking state, the individual does not enjoy the benefits of actions and thoughts in dream state. In other words, the individual is not consciously a party to the thoughts thought or to the acts done in dream. Hence, he is free from merits and demerits. Even if he murders somebody else or has unethical contacts with others or with kith and kin, it will not end in sin. Righteous acts also will not earn any merit to him. Hence, no fate or kanmam results. In that respect, **dream state is superior to waking state.**

This superior concept may be applied to waking state, if the individual disowns the benefits that he may reap from his good thoughts and actions. If it is bad on him, he must suffer without complaining. In simple words, the individual with wisdom will be *indifferent* to both good and bad happenings in life. In other words, the good and bad acts will not snow ball into karma provided we disown the fruits of good and bad acts.

The more dominant fear that we get in waking state, directly or indirectly, is the fear of losing Life. The fear that we get in dream is also based on the same fact but it will be, somewhat, stronger.

In deep sleep state, the mind is in a brief sojourn in Life and hence, the individual enjoys only the joyful and blissful state. Here, the nature of the mind is not explicit but the nature of Life. The nature of Life is only a joyous state but of mind it is both joy and grief.

The waking state where the individual experiences only the blissful state is in Samadhi state. It is a state where the individual's mind is in conscious state but his body is dead to his senses and to the environment. One can attain this state in deep meditation. Meditation is a state where the mind is wholly in union with Life or concentrated on something else. In real Samadhi state, mind almost dissolves in Life/ knowledge and in that condition, Atman is pure without three gunas. The same can also be obtained by devotion to God (Bhakthi) where the individual, being engrossed in God, is mute to his senses and to the external environment. The bliss can also be experienced in normal waking state provided the individual's mind is completely absorbed and detached from the thoughts and acts or simply, detached from the world.

Human being or any other being can involve themselves in physical activities only with physical or gross body. With physical body, he earns karma by owning the benefits until death, which is unavoidable.

*Mortal indeed is this body, held by death. But **it is the support of this deathless bodiless Atman.** Verily, the embodied self is held by pleasure and pain. Surely, there is no cessation of pleasure and pain for the one who is embodied or with a body. Both pleasure and pain do not, indeed, touch the one who is bodiless. – (Chandogya Upanishad 8:12:1)*

He that loveth his life shall lose it; and he that hateth his life in this world shall keep it unto life eternal, says Jesus Christ – John 12:25.

Therefore, when an Atman takes a body using insentient food materials, it will be subjected to both pleasure and pain. There is no way out. When it discards the mind along with body, the Atman will be in eternal bliss with no pain and displeasure i.e., it becomes Brahman.

The knowers of Brahman or Brahmacarins who have purified their mind through the withdrawal of the senses and other means see everywhere of ancient One who is the seed of the universe – (Chandogya Upanishad 3:17:7)

Subtlety

Subtlety plays a major part in the creation and operation of the universe. The universe itself is in two forms – subtle and physical forms. It is something that the scientists are totally unaware of. Most probably, it is due to the fact that they do not know the real nature and significance of the subtle state of human body in dream state. We or scientists give no credence to the dream state. Nonetheless, it is beyond any experimentation. Experimentation may be possible at the level of physical state but not at subtle state.

According to Vedas, the five major elements namely the space, the air, the fire, the water, and the earth themselves were first made in subtle forms and then into physical form by mixing the subtle forms in a definite proportion. *The contradictory and at the same time complementary gunas are imparted even at the stage of subtle formation.*

Now, let us again consider the dream state that we experience during the intermediate states of waking state and deep dreamless state. This intermediate dream state is experienced to a large extent by those who are unable to get into deep sleep state. Whatever it is, dream state is experienced by all. This is the reality. Nobody can deny this fact.

In dream state, we do get our physical body and we do experience with our senses what we experience in waking state. In dream state we do see, hear, smell, taste, and feel the touch. Of these, the touch feel is the strongest and especially when the individual is involved in sex activities in dream, he ejaculates physically! As already said, in dream state, we get the body as we have in waking state but in subtle form. Is it not a puzzle that we see without the physical eye; hear without the physical ear; feel the touch without the physical skin; taste without the physical tongue; and smell without the physical nose? How do we experience them? Think of it. Is it *Maya* or a wonder?

Why do we get a dream state? It is also to indicate that subtlety state exists. Our body is an inanimate or insentient thing but animated by Life. When Life/Atman departs, the body which is made of insentient food materials is left behind. This body is the one that we get in dream state but in subtle form. *Dream is the only meaningful proof for the existence of subtle state.* So, **definitely** the subtle state exists. There is no doubt in it. It is something like *we can see the activities of a ghost in a possessed person but not the ghost.* Hence, insentient things exist in subtle form also.

What the scientists are doing? They are just probing the physical state of matter and not the subtle state of matter. They can never probe the subtle state because it is beyond their scope. But scientists can create wonder things that are amazing using the subtlety of matter unknowingly. Even the scientists are amazed by the work of what we call as silicon chips, transistors, etc. In these, what we feed physically (such as in computers, smart phones, robots) is stored subtly i.e., in the subtle state of matter. What is stored subtly we get back physically. With improved versions, we can store any amount of information in a subtle form of matter. Even memory is a subtle form in living beings. There is, in fact, no limit. Such is the power of subtlety.

The wonderful work of television, computers, smart phones, robots, and whatever the amazing job such instruments do, we just make use of subtle form of them without any knowledge of it. But we boast of them? In one way, the boasting is correct because scientists are able to find a way to harness subtle power even though they are unaware of it. It is definitely a great achievement to harness the subtle power even without knowing it. Harnessing the subtle power is made possible as we get more and more into the smaller sizes of subatomic particles. I think it is also a mercy of 'God'. What is behind this subtlety? Who works behind subtlety? Think over it.

The wonderful nature of subtlety is its connectivity. Subtle bodies can have connection with one another irrespective of distance of separation. Though the physical body may remain stationary, its subtle form can travel at a speed greater than the speed of light because it harbors no mass or it can get its presence anywhere instantly. It is simply not bounded. Why and how subatomic particles such as photon (of light) travel at a faster speed is itself a great wonder. The particles, smaller than photon, should have a speed faster than light and they can have variable speeds or remain stationary and that is why Life/God is **omnipotent**. There is also an inexplicable unknown way/type of connection, through which subtle bodies can communicate instantly (something like telepathy). In subtle state nothing is impossible. When God contacts his devotee, through dream subtly, the dream may become vivid and memorable on waking. Or, if God wishes the dream to be memorable, it will become memorable to the individual. God's domain is in subtle state which extends into physical state. Physical state can be controlled through subtle state but not *vice versa but with some exceptions!*

Subtlety needs probabilistic thinking to understand because anything is possible in subtle state. Subtle state cannot be bound by the laws of physics nor will they be confined within the mathematical treatment. Physics laws may be more applicable to those which are greater in size than subatomic particles.

Mind work is much more powerful than physical work. Mind is subtle. Therefore, it is more powerful. This subtle power was used through *mantras* on olden days. Through *mantras* they achieved many things - Rama in Ramayana, Arjuna in Mahabharata, and so many others used their weapons infused with the subtle power invoking the Lord of the particular subtle power and thus, they did wonders with their weapons.

A banyan tree is buried subtly in its seed. A human being is buried subtly in the zygote, the fertilized egg. A plant is buried subtly in its parts also i.e., a part of the plant may grow into the plant. There is nothing without subtlety. God works only through subtlety. If we don't believe in subtlety which **exists**, we cannot believe in God. Though God is not easily realizable, he can be realized with his grace or mercy but that needs a mind that is pure. God's grace is the only way to realize God. His grace will take shape in a pure mind. That is why devotees with pure heart pleaded or plead for the grace or mercy of God. They plead even for a pure mind.

All this subtlety and physicality of matter will vanish when the universe is dissolved and what will remain is the so-called dark emptiness filled with Life particle (Brahman), subtle of the subtler. Re-creation of the universe may take place after crores of years or yugas. Who knows all these? In short, *the universe is the visible form of the invisible Atman*. Hence, the universe is also termed as mayai or illusion.

Everything in This Universe is of Light (Fire) Form – Science

Atman is of light form. Effulgent Atman is the fundamental unit in the creation of universe. Hence, everything in the universe is of light or fire form. Whenever the term light is mentioned, we must remember that it is associated with thermal energy. (*That is why Isvara is said to be of fire form*). It follows that all insentient beings or things are of light or fire form but curtailed. The light in things is curtailed may be at the atomic stage or below it. Why is it curtailed? If light is not curtailed in things, we cannot see them clearly and handling is also not possible because of the thermal energy of light. But everything is of light form and it will become clear if we go to the subatomic stage of things. Above and below the atomic stage, the things may take up (or absorb) or release thermal energy or may remain in between. In short, everything is of light (or fire) form. One more wonder is that there may be expression of light with less or no perceivable thermal energy or heat may be expressed with less light or no perceivable light.

A wonderful thing in this universe, no doubt, is light. We know all religions invariably claim

God is of light form (i.e., God in Atman state). Light has been the primary tool for perceiving the world.

The other wonderful thing is **sound.** In Sanskrit philology, the relation between *sabda* (sound) and *artha* (object) is considered inseparable. This is something to be pondered over. Actually, sound is the first wonderful thing because it can bring about changes physically, mentally, and even spiritually. It affects the mind either advantageously or disadvantageously. It connects the people. Languages are the products of sound. **It is virtually formless.** It is produced when objects vibrate. This vibration produces vibrations in the surrounding medium. The vibrations, thus produced, transmit the sound further through medium. Human ear picks up the sound intact. Sound may be audible, inaudible, unpleasant, pleasant, soft, loud, noisy, musical, and more. The varieties of sound seem to be countless and puzzling. Sound can be considered as **a true subtle form** but expressed audibly. Light offers itself to understand the universe. So far, the mystery of light itself is not fully known. However, the effect of light has been extensively studied but not of the sound. Sound, in the form of mantras, can communicate with the subtle state and one can achieve anything. Sound is not a physical entity and hence it may not be possible to know more about it.

The pleasing aspect of sound is music. It can also be said as delightful. The melody of songs is certainly delightful to the ear and the heart. Heavenly melody lifts one to the highest divine experience in the opinion of Yajnavalkya, the saint.

Both *stotra* and sastra hymns and *mantras* (in short words) are full of sound and they serve to create contact with God. Samaveda, one of the four Vedas is known for its musical form. The songs of great devotees have the same effect.

Auspicious sounds will hasten to him (Isvara, the inner dweller of sun) *and continue to delight him –* (Chandogya Upanishad – 3:19:4)

He, who knows the actual play of vina or veena (harp like), the ancient musical instrument of Indian subcontinent and an expert in the science of melody and time with pure melting heart, easily attains salvation.

Coming to light again, there are insentient things that emit light energy easily. There are things which emit light energy when caused to emit. All things almost emit light below the atomic stage. The behavior of subatomic particles follows quantum mechanics/physics as put forward by scientists.

The laws of **classical physics** may be applicable up to the molecule level. Even in the case of particles sticking together (in general loosely) to form bigger particles, the properties go on changing from coarse particles to individual molecules through colloidal and nano-particle sizes. Group of molecules may exist in three general forms namely solid, liquid, and gas depending upon molecular interactions (attraction and repulsion) and temperature. When the sizes are atomic or subatomic range, the quantum effects dominate and we call it as **quantum physics**. It is said that the analysis of the frequencies of light emitted and absorbed by atoms was a principal impetus for the wonderful development of quantum mechanics. In quantum physics, the laws of classical physics may lose its significance to a greater extent. Even if new laws are postulated or mathematically treated in quantum physics, it has to be based, to some extent, on probabilistic thinking. There may be uncertainty with respect to laws of physics but not with nature's way of operation.

Let us not delve into it deeply because the behavior of Nature below the subatomic levels seems to be ambiguous as well as awesome and to have no limitations. It seems to have unimaginable as well as wonderful properties that are perplexing and any demarcation has to be probabilistic or becomes untenable.

The point which I want to stress here is that the universe is filled with Life particles something like water molecules filling the bulk of the liquid water. Because of subtle nature of Life particles, the space filled by them presents a vacuum-like condition. It is virtually inert-like and dark not exhibiting light and unaffected but at the same time supporting, causing, directing, and executing all activities of universe in an indiscernible manner i.e., as if something absent operates.

*He (Brahman), again, **is the** bringer **or vehicle (carrier) of light**.* (Chandogya Upanishad 4:15:4) There is no such state called absolute vacuum in the universe. Every act and thing are supported by it. Whether this notion will bring out a paradigm shift in understanding of light and the universe is up to the physicists. Life is subtler. Subtle of the subtler is knowledge.

Everything in this universe seems to be quantized. As a general rule, only from quantized particles atoms are formed by combination. And from combinations of atoms, particles (molecules) with so much of variations are formed. The properties of subatomic particles seem to be astounding. As the particles become smaller and smaller, the properties go on changing drastically and the wonderful functions of subtle state (such as storage of information) start to manifest.

The other aspect of subatomic particles is that when the particles get into subatomic size, speed (or movement) becomes an inherent property. Whether electromagnetic property alone can do this trick or whether it has that effect at subatomic level is to be pondered over. However, the speed (momentum) associated with electromagnetic property is advantageously used in telecommunication technology which has changed the world dramatically to the present state. Light is said to contain particles called photons which have been found to travel at a speed of about 300,000 km/sec through the so-called vacuum. Neutrino particles, which are considered to be lighter (or probably smaller) than photon, is believed to travel faster than light. From this it can be inferred that as the size becomes smaller and smaller, the speed of the particle becomes greater and greater. The speed of Life particle, whose size is said to be atom of atom in subtle state, is greater than the speed of mind which in turn is so many times greater than the speed of light as mentioned in Vedas. It is instantaneous. But at the same time, the speed may be variable or nil in accordance with the medium. That is the versatility of Life particle as claimed by Vedas because it is subtle, omniscient and hence omnipotent.

Scientists can remain satisfied with the research on physicality of matter and can utilize to some extent the functions of subtlety of matter to their advantage but the subtlety of matter can never be known. They can just find a way to harness the power and functions of subtlety to the extent possible. This harnessing of subtle power itself is or will be a greatest achievement.

Einstein, a great physicist born in Germany was of the opinion that nothing can travel faster than light. He reasoned that the mass will increase tremendously with speed and hence, automatically it will be decelerated. I think Einstein would have accepted that there may be something which is faster than light provided he knew something about subtlety (of things).

There has been a lot of talk about *spooky action at a distance* or quantum entanglement in physics world and also about *double-slit experiment*. Even in this decade, they are being experimented. Quantum physics is an area of physics that deals with subatomic particles. It is said that entangled particles can effectively exchange information instantaneously. It is a phenomenon by which one particle can effectively know something about another particle instantaneously even if the particles are separated by a great distance, say thousands of light years. Physicists can harness such spooky action at a distance with subatomic particles. This spooky action itself is related to subtlety of matter. Double-slit experiment remains a weird one or phenomenon for scientists.

Einstein, regarded as a great scientist of his century, has expressed this quantum physics as, **"God does not play dice"**. I think this is a well said statement even without knowing its real significance. God definitely does not play with uncertainty. It is true because the siddhars or rishis on those days were able to tell correctly what is in store for an individual in future. They were able to be present at two different places at the same time. They were able to communicate with some other who was far away and for that I am unable to think whether they needed such quantum entanglement. They were able to travel to far off places in a trice. The travel is made possible because of subtlety of body and then materializing themselves at the place desired. Time and distance are no bar for those who have realized themselves. A devout devotee, good in heart, can even put off a fire that occurs somewhere at a far-off place. Such is the power of subtlety. In Mahabharata, it is said that the charioteer of the king Dhiritarashtra of Hastinapura, by name Sanjaya, was able to see and narrate the events as well as the conversation that happened at the battle-field at a far-off place called Kurukshetra, as if we see the happenings at a far-off place live in television. God simply obeys his devotee, Vyasa, who wrote Mahabharata, conferred Sanjaya with the power of seeing the happenings at the battle-field. What a great concern God has for his devotee! God becomes a slave to his slave or like a father to his little child. Even the miracles performed by devotees are by the mercy of God within them. **Jesus is a great example *and he did so many miracles with the mercy of God*.** In God's domain there are no uncertainties or probabilities. If it is there, God cannot control the whole universe. ***This uncertainty encountered in quantum physics is due to the lack of knowledge about the subtlety of Nature.*** When subtlety comes into play, the scientists have to resort to uncertainties or probabilities.

However, it will be amazing if the scientists find a way in future to harness this effect further and therefore the use of quantum entanglement and also about the double-slit experiment **even without knowing about the subtlety of Nature** to their advantage. And who knows that it may also pave the way for knowing more about Nature. But how long will it take? God only knows! In my opinion, it will come to fruition when God decides favorably and it was also so with fundamental inventions and discoveries so far made. It may be evident if you can closely understand the time and situations when such great inventions and discoveries were made. Messengers (those destined to be so) are sent to set the mind in the right perspective and to say about the existence of God and in the same way, the scientists are sent to probe the universe and to harness the functions of insentient things to the uplift of living style. In fact, the probing nature of spiritualists and scientists may look contradictory but the end will turn out to be the same. The universe is really a wonderful thing! The Nature seems to allow the growth of science. Who knows what more mysteries await the scientific world!

The size of ultimate fundamental building unit for the creation of universe must be of a size that no other particle is smaller than this. This size is given approximately as 5×10^{-41} meter by the great siddhar Thirumoor in Thirumandrum. That is, the size is as minute as to be considered as subtle of the subtler. That means it has no mass. It occupies virtually no space. It forms the so-called empty space or so-called vacuum. One cannot say it is matter or energy. Simply, it is nothing but something. That something is Life in infinitesimal fraction of knowledge – that is limitless like Space. Can anyone assign a size for Life in terms of knowledge? That is why Vedas say Brahman is infinite. Infinite is happiness.

The universe has come up from Life particle. The versatility of Life 'particle' with unlimited knowledge is incomprehensible. Life is sat (existence or being), knowledge, and bliss. **It becomes God in Atman state** to rule over the universe or whatever created. Life/Brahman will remain ever as an observer or **witness**.

Let us again remember what the Upanishads said about Atman. What is applicable to Atman is applicable to Life 'particles.' In fact, what is applicable to Life is applicable to Atman.

This self (Atman) *is one unmoving. It is faster than mind. Having preceded this mind, it is beyond the reach of the senses. Ever ready, it outstrips all that run* (including light). *By its mere presence, it enables the activities of living beings* (and also insentient things).

It moves, and it moves not. it is far, and it is near. It is within all this (the existing inanimate and animate beings of the universe) *and it is also outside all this* (i.e., the space outside)

The Kada or Kata Upanishad says,

This Atman is atom of atom size (very minute and subtle). *Hence, it is not attainable by debate -* (1:2:8). That is, it is beyond debate.

This Atman, sitting or lying down, can go anywhere – (1:2:20).

From the above statements, we can understand the versatility of Life 'particles' which fill the Space as well serve as the constituent of invisible and visible things in the universe. There is no such hard and fast rule to contain Life 'particle'. As the Life particle is subtle, it is able to communicate instantaneously and go through any medium. Moreover, Life 'particles' are identical with each other and same and what one particle knows is instantaneously known to the particle that is at a great distance (say innumerable light years away). Nothing can move without its knowledge because it is the one that moves. Whatever happens in sentient or insentient beings is only according to its discretion (which depends on karma with respect to living beings) because it is the one that executes. Simply everything is Life or Brahman.

I think the particles in the universe may be put into three categories or levels.

1. At and above atomic and molecular level

2. Subatomic level

3. Subtle level

Particles of Atomic and Molecular Level

Atoms of elements have their unique properties. Molecules formed by combination or interaction of atoms have entirely different properties from the properties of individual atoms of which the molecules or compounds are made. The molecules thus formed contribute to the great percentage of the bulk of the world. They comprise the insentient things. They also have wave property but too insignificant to be perceived.

All the non-moving living beings (vegetation) make use of the atoms and the molecules of different elements for their growth and produce. The vegetation and their produce are the ultimate food materials for the moving living beings for their growth. Thus, the insentient and sentient forms constitute the world. In them, the subtle state is not explicit. But the functions of the subtle state are being harnessed unknowingly.

Subatomic Level of Particles

In subatomic particles, the electromagnetic power makes them to have some wonderful and unimaginable properties. They are considered to have the duality of being particle and wave.

This property of duality is said to be shared by all the primary constituents of Nature. Science world has benefited so much by making use of electromagnetic properties of them. Electrons are said to have spin. Imagine the size of an electron and even with that size it is said to have spin. Is it imaginable? Advancement in science is exemplary. Massless subatomic particles have a unique property of speed. The speed of light (photon) particles has been described as the maximum speed attainable through the so-called vacuum. Making use of this speed and electromagnetic property to some extent possible, the telecommunication technology is doing wonders. It has brought about a colossal change in this world. All the computers, smart phones, robots, and any instrument with amazing functions are only due to the subatomic particles. The physics of subatomic particles itself has been named as *quantum physics or quantum mechanics* apart from classical physics.

Nearly 200 subatomic particles have been reported to be detected and there may be more to be detected or may remain undetected for ever. Only the subatomic particles in the atom are being exploited to the greater extent possible. Scientists are baffled with some properties of subatomic particles such as quantum entanglement and double-slit experiment and even some other aspects of Nature. What is in store will also prove to be wonderful in future. Encryption and quantum computers may make their way strongly because of subtle power inherent with physical state. The scientists may find a way to harness the wonderful subtle power even without knowing it. That is, **they can find a way to harness the effects but not the cause.** The amazing properties of subatomic particles are only due to their subtle state, of which the scientists are **totally ignorant.**

Subtle Level

Subtle level cannot be known or described. It is better to just say Life as well as Life in the form of Atman is subtle in nature. It may be described as subtle of the subtler as given in Vedas. These are in pure subtle form. Simply, it is omnipresent, omniscient, and omnipotent.

Inference

The universe has evolved from only **one thing and that is the indestructible ever-existing Life.** That means 'the visible as well as the invisible complicated world' has blossomed from the invisible, subtle, and conscious life 'particles' through the wholeness or perfect Atman state. There are **individual infinite Atmans** becoming the living beings and **finite combined Atmans** with *curtailed consciousness and light* forming non-living insentient beings. They unite into a living being with a body. **There is no absolute vacuum. There is no absolute insentient thing also.** The universe(s) forms only a part of the Space. The Space including the space occupied by the universe is filled with Life 'particles'. Hence, Life is Space and Space is Life. Life is an abstract intelligence and hence, it has no source. Life is also called **'Sat or Brahman'**. Brahman is knowledge and Bliss. In short, without any name, it is Existence, Knowledge, and Bliss. Before Life becomes Atman, it remains dark. It takes up light form in Atman state. Vedas especially the Upanishads have elaborated exclusively or mostly about Atman depicting it as Brahman or God Isvara. By discarding the three bodies and thus the three gunas, an **individual becomes Brahman** i.e., he attains liberation through God Isvara.

Simply saying, the aspiring individual (i.e., his Atman) becomes the infinite by discarding the finite (i.e., the body)

Conclusion

Life is **The Supreme Being** or **The Supreme God** which is **infinite, minute of the minutest, incomprehensible,** and **undefinable.** Instead of saying as minute of the minutest, it may be said as transcendental as well as infinitesimal fraction of consciousness. Simply, it is the intelligent principle. It has a surpassing wonderful power and its authority is incontrovertible. It is the only one that exists as Space and has become the ever-dynamic universe (or universes) and whatever beyond it. We, including Gods, Devas, Rakshas (demons), and all moving and non-moving living beings are all the incarnations of the **Supreme Being**. The difference in the incarnations, with respect to living beings, is only due to the karma earned because of freedom or freewill given to the individual Atman. The universe (or universes) in its insentient form is nothing but the manifestation of the **Supreme Being**. Is it not a great unfathomable (or even unimaginable) wonder that Life, a tenuous consciousness, which cannot be seen but inferred, has become the insentient cosmos with all its sentient beings?

Life alone is unchanging and all that are formed by association or combination of invisible and subtle Life '*particles*' are liable to change. Life, the supreme reality, creates (in fact, becomes) gods to rule over the universe.

Shiva, Vishnu, Yahweh, Allah or any other name given by any other religion are just the difference in the names of God. Such name differences are not properly understood. We must also know that **we, although influenced by regional or Geographical variations in this world are all the products or descendants of a single source** or **the children of God.** All the names and forms of both living (or sentient) beings and non-living (or insentient) beings are of God. When it is so, why should we hate and fight with each other. No country is self-sufficient in all respects. Let every country be content with the existing territory and live with exchange of necessities of the growing civilization with rapid advancement in science. Let the affluent country/people provide the have-nots to erase out famine or starving. If we **live** like this **with love**, what is there to be afraid of.